Abundance of the Heart

Julia A. Royston

ROYSTON
Publishing

BK Royston Publishing
Jeffersonville IN
http://bkroystonpublishing.com
bkroystonpublishing@gmail.com

© 2024

All Rights Reserved. No part of this book may be reproduced, stored in a retrieval system, or transmitted by any means without the written permission of the author.

Cover and Layout: BK Royston Publishing

Good News Translation (GNT) - (Today's English Version, Second Edition) © 1992 American Bible Society. All rights reserved. For more information about GNT, visit www.bibles.com and www.gnt.bible.

King James Version (KJV) — Public Domain

New International Version (NIV) - Holy Bible, New International Version®, NIV® Copyright ©1973,

ISBN-13: 978-1-963136-45-6

Printed in the United States of America

Dedication

I dedicate this book as a reminder that it's the Heart that Matters Most.

The Heart

Search It.

Clean It.

Follow It.

Theme Scripture

Luke 6:45 (KJV)

A good man out of the good treasure of his heart bringeth forth that which is good; and an evil man out of the evil treasure of his heart bringeth forth that which is evil: for of the abundance of the heart his mouth speaketh.

Acknowledgements

I thank my Lord and Savior Jesus Christ for giving me another opportunity to introduce more people to you. I thank you for entrusting this gift to me. Lord, let your Spirit move, guide and empower through this book to the people who will read it.

To my husband, Brian K. Royston, the love of my life for loving and cheering me on so much that I can be and do all that God has placed in me. I love you.

To my Mom, my greatest supporter and best friend. To my Dad, who is in heaven, whom I know is proud of me and always encouraged me to go for it. Thanks to all the rest of my family for their love and support.

A special thank you to Rev. and Mrs. Claude R. Royston for their love and support.

To the rest of my clients, friends and family, thank you and love you always. Let's go!

Love, Julia

Table of Contents

Dedication	iii
Theme Scripture	iv
Acknowledgements	v
Introduction	xi
The Pure in Heart	1
The Heart Is Desperately Wicked	5
A Hard Heart	9
The Heart Can Get Dirty	13
The Treasure Inside Your Heart	17
The Wise Heart	21
What's Been Added to Your Heart?	25
Hate Is In the Heart	29
Faint Heart	33
Discouragement of the Heart	37
The Heart Thinks	41
The Heart Talks	45

Pride in Your Heart	49
The Heart is Stubborn	53
Gladness of Heart	57
Call the Doctor—The Heart Is Sick	61
Call 911! Now It's the Head and the Heart	65
Loving With NO Heart	69
The Heart Hears and Decides	73
Comfort Your Heart	77
Grieve the Heart	81
Alot in the Heart	85
Serve With Your Heart	89
The Heart of a Lion	93
An Understanding Heart	97
After God's Own Heart	101
A New Heart	105
A Stony Heart	109
Guard Your Heart	113
Set Your Heart	117
An Undivided Heart	121

An Unprepared Heart	125
The Heart of the King	129
The Heart That Lives Forever	133
The Troubled Heart	137
The Strengthened Heart	141
The Designer Heart	145
The Law Is in the Heart	149
A Fixed Heart	153
The Broken Heart	157
About the Author	161
More Books by this Author	163

Introduction

Inspiration can come from many places. Don't talk to a real creative long because ideas will start to come just throughout the conversation.

For this book, it was different. Normally, God will speak to me about a topic and give me specific instructions but these instructions came a different way. My husband is a techie, plain and simple. He loves everything about technology and the new AI (Artificial Intelligence) is no different. He wants to learn how it works, benefits and most importantly, which I love about him, how he can help me in my business. He put in a prompt and the heart on the cover was created. Now, let me say the rest of the book's text is MINE. Don't get it twisted. I love technology but I still love the creative process.

I saw the heart and God says, "Create and write a devotional about the heart."

I said, "okay, 21 devotionals sound good and quicker or maybe 30."

God said, "No, do 40."

I did my first search and didn't realize all that God's word says about the heart. It was a labor of love, learning and understanding. I pray that you are blessed by them and impacted as I am.

Let's go!

How is Your Heart?

The Pure in Heart

Matthew 5:8 (KJV)
"Blessed are the pure in heart: for they shall see God."

In our society today, there are so many fake, replacement, and organic ingredients in our food that we really don't know what we're eating. So, what's pure? You really don't know what's pure unless you grow it, prepare it, cook it, and eat it with your hands. Jesus said that if you keep a pure heart, you will see God. It's a daily task to keep evil and unclean things out of your heart as well as imitation and false things trying to enter your life. Work on keeping a pure heart. I believe that you're not only going to see God in Heaven, but you'll see God's hand, His handy work, and His purpose fulfilled in your life right here on earth. That is if you keep your heart pure towards and about the things of God.

Check your heart. Is it pure, or has it gotten a little dirty?

It's your decision.

Notes from the Heart

_____
_____
_____
_____
_____
_____
_____
_____
_____
_____
_____
_____
_____
_____
_____
_____
_____
_____
_____
_____
_____
_____

Notes from the Heart

The Heart Is Desperately Wicked

Jeremiah 17:9 (KJV)
"The **heart** is deceitful above all things
and desperately wicked:
Who can know it?"

The heart is deceitful above all things, and desperately wicked are harsh words. Being deceitful is a deal breaker for me. I will walk away at the slightest hint that you are purposely trying to get over on me. My "Daddy didn't raise no fool." I will not stand by and allow anyone to take advantage of me. I will leave the money on the table, block you, and delete you. I can still love you from afar.

The scripture says the heart is deceitful in that it can cause you to believe something one way when, in fact, it isn't that way at all. On the other hand, not only can it deceive you, but it is also desperately wicked. In this scripture, if left to the heart's own devices, it can and will be desperately wicked. That's the reason why you have to keep your heart clean and pure at all times. On its own, without the work of the Holy Spirit convicting and changing you, it will become desperately wicked. Who can know it? Only God. Only God can truly know. He will try, inspect, and give a proper conclusion of what's actually going on in your heart. It is not the cardiologist, but only God truly knows your heart.

Notes from the Heart

_____
_____
_____
_____
_____
_____
_____
_____
_____
_____
_____
_____
_____
_____
_____
_____
_____
_____
_____
_____

Notes from the Heart

_____
_____
_____
_____
_____
_____
_____
_____
_____
_____
_____
_____
_____
_____
_____
_____
_____
_____
_____
_____
_____

A Hard Heart

Exodus 7:13 (KJV)
"And he hardened Pharaoh's heart…"

As a teacher, I would give soft playdough to the kids to mold, make, and create. They had so much fun; there was minor cleanup after the activity. The kids enjoyed touching something other than paper and pencil. They weren't being quizzed, graded, and penalized for something according to state standards. It was time to be imaginative and creative. However, there was nothing worse than when the playdough got old; somebody left the top off, and it was too hard to work with. No more fun or funny, multicolored shapes. It was just hard dough that was no longer sticky enough to even play with.

Did you know that your heart can be hard, no fun, not pliable, or moldable to be used by God? Your heart can get so hard that very few people are tolerant of wanting to work with you or spend their spare, fun time with you. They would shun you unless forced to be involved. Why? You're mean. You're critical most of the time and can see no one's side but your own. In Exodus, God made Pharaoh's heart hard.

Sometimes, God makes your boss' heart hard against you to move you to another department or out of the company altogether. Sometimes, God makes your heart hard to drive other people from you so He can talk to you, change you and then, once changed, use you for His glory.

I want my heart to remain soft, pliable, and usable for God's glory. Don't you? Don't let your heart can be hardened by the cares and problems of this world, and only God can work with that heart.

Notes from the Heart

The Heart Can Get Dirty

Proverbs 20:9 (KJV)
"Who can say, I have made my **heart** clean, I am pure from my sin?"

In most households, a weekly task is doing laundry. Our clothes pile up and get dirty; weekly, detergent is used along with fabric softener, bleach, or another solvent to remove stubborn stains. Dishes are washed daily. The trash goes out every other day or more. And we should clean ourselves daily. Throughout our lives and the world, cleanliness is a part of our lifestyle.

What do we need to clean our heart and purify it from sin? The blood of Jesus is the best bleaching agent. Naturally, our heart just adds more stains, but miraculously, Jesus' blood cleanses.

Secondly, reading, applying and obeying the Word of God daily. We can't do it on our own. We can't do it ourselves because we were born in sin and shaped in iniquity. Who can say I made my own heart clean and purified myself from sin? Not me. Only through the blood of Jesus, applying the Word, and the power of the Holy Spirit are we made clean. Furthermore, that cleansing is daily. It's time to take another bath!

Let's go!

Notes from the Heart

Notes from the Heart

The Treasure Inside Your Heart

Matthew 6:21 (KJV)
"For where your treasure is, there will your **heart** be also."

When I think of treasure, I think of pirates and bounty hunters looking for gold with a map. There are modern-day bounty hunters and treasure seekers as well. What do you treasure? Are you willing to seek after it like a pirate? Willing to risk it all for the treasure you seek? I hear people say yes but realize when there is no action that they "don't have the heart for it." This statement is multilayered and we will focus on the meaning. You don't have the heart for something because it is NOT of value to you. The scripture says, where the treasure is, that is where your heart is also. That thing, person, or place that you value is where your heart IS. You are passionate about it. You will risk all for it. You will seek out information, find resources, pay for a coach, get a mentor, stay up late, and rise early for it.

Where your treasure is, that's where your heart is and your body will be there too.

What do you treasure?

Notes from the Heart

_____
_____
_____
_____
_____
_____
_____
_____
_____
_____
_____
_____
_____
_____
_____
_____
_____
_____
_____
_____

Notes from the Heart

The Wise Heart

Exodus 28:3 (KJV)
"And thou shalt speak unto all that are wise hearted…"

There is a time and place for everything. In a crisis, emergency, or a life-changing problem, you need wisdom. Laughter, jokes, or being playful has its place, and we need that too. But in difficult times, you need a serious person with knowledge and wisdom. Exodus advises us to not only speak to a wise human being but also speak to a human being who has a wise heart. A wise hearted person has wisdom inside them. Hopefully, that person will advise, speak, exhort, and teach from their wise heart. Nothing is worse than someone with an agenda that doesn't fit the moment, occasion, or season.

Rather than focus on the people, surroundings, or needs at the time, they are only focused on themselves and their agenda. Wise-hearted people see God to know the correct time, place, and way to reason to say and do important things.

Lord, give us wisdom and a wise heart to meet the needs of Your people and do Your perfect will.

Notes from the Heart

Notes from the Heart

What's Been Added to Your Heart?

Exodus 35:34 (KJV)
"And he hath put in his **heart**..."

I don't cook much. When I use a recipe, I clearly follow it. My husband, on the other hand, loves cooking and using recipes but he's also gets excited about experimenting with foods.

When trying new foods, he often says, "I can do that but I would do this or that to it." From that point on, he makes those foods into his own personal cooking style and flavor. He adds a little of this or a little of that to the recipe, and if he doesn't have a specific ingredient, he knows how to improvise so the dish tastes just as good or better than the original. He is excellent at it! I have the body to prove it.

The ingredients you use in a specific recipe are a choice. You decide. No one can make you put ground beef in a recipe if you want to add ground chicken or tofu instead. It is the same with your heart; with the help of the Holy Spirit, you can choose what to add or not add to your heart.

Only add what tastes good, is beneficial and makes you healthy.

Notes from the Heart

Notes from the Heart

Hate Is In the Heart

Leviticus 19:17 (KJV)
"Thou shalt not hate thy brother in thine **heart**:"

The heart has always been and will be the symbol of love. It is traditionally used in February on Valentine's Day, at anniversaries, and the list goes on and on. However, what happens when hate creeps in? The symbol of love, the heart, is just a symbol and not reality. In Leviticus, there is a warning for us. It is a commandment in this verse to not to hate your brother. Now, in the New Testament, James states that if you don't love, which is hate, you don't know God. The objective here is to warn, command, and employ you to NOT hate your brother because your heart should have love residing for your brother and mankind.

Why? God is love and NOT hate. The two commandments of all time are to love God and then love your neighbor, which includes your brother, just like you love yourself. Every commandment, including this one, is subjected to the love commandments. Now, on the other hand, it didn't state that there might not be a reason for you to hate your brother. Or maybe your brother did something to deserve to be hated. Regardless, you still don't hate him. Even if there is a valid reason to hate, don't hate him. You can be mad at him; just don't hate him. You might need to separate for a season; don't let that hate get down in your heart. It will require God's love to keep that hate out, but the true essence of GOD is love. He's got enough love for you and the world, plus not lose one drop from Himself.

Find a way to love and fight to keep out hate.

Notes from the Heart

Faint Heart

Leviticus 26:36 (KJV)
"And upon them that are left alive of you I will send a faintness into their hearts…"

Entrepreneurship is NOT for the faint of heart. I have said it many times. The struggles, determination, vision, work, effort, and risk of entrepreneurship will try and test every fiber of your being. If you are not strong enough, you will stop, close, or shut down the business. Some people leave that particular industry altogether because it took so much from them. The requirements FROM them were too much to continue. You've got to know what your limits, boundaries, and risk management are for your life. It's not for everyone.

In business, there are also contracts and agreements that should not only be signed, dated, and copied but must also be completed and obeyed. In Leviticus 26, God sends His children His contract with the requirements of what He expects. He also says what will happen if they obey. The obedience part is wonderful, but if they don't obey Him and do what He requires, it is not pretty. There are severe punishments. In verse 36, He says He will send a faintness into their hearts. Now, that sounds harsh, but the contract requirements were delivered from the beginning in verse 1. In verse 36, He states, "I am going to cause your heart to faint." You will be fearful, scared and run at the slightest sound of a leaf. Nobody will even be chasing you, but you will run. He did it because you didn't obey.

If you obey Him, your heart will run well and you enjoy all of God's benefits and blessings He has for your life.

Notes from the Heart

Discouragement of the Heart

Numbers 32:7 (KJV)
"And wherefore discourage ye
the **heart** of the children of Israel."

Most things God asks you to do will require you to risk everything. It takes BIG faith and courage to do it. We walk by faith. The just shall live by faith. But when Joshua took over from Moses after his death, God specifically and twice in the same verse said to be strong and courageous. The root of the word courageous is courage. The opposite of courage is to discourage. In chapter 32 of Numbers, Moses was still alive, and the children of Israel hadn't arrived to the promised land yet. They were almost there but had to cross the Jordan River next. Two tribes, Gad and Reuben, said, "We don't want to go over there because the land is best over here for our cattle. We don't want to go over there and fight with our brethren. We'll just enjoy life over here."

People can see the struggle you're about to go through, but they don't get the vision God gave explicitly to you. Remember, the promised land was given to all of the tribes of Israel that were alive, not just to ten but to all twelve. God was with them, but they would still have to fight. The fight was okay if all twelve were going to fight, but not when two tribes of fighters were missing. Moses told these two tribes, "You discourage your brethren when you're unwilling to go and fight for the land that was given to you also. You want to stay back and let them do all of the fighting, and their heart will be discouraged at the start because they are not fighting with the full army and everyone that could fight on board."

Have you ever faced that same type of situation? Your heart is in it and strengthened when you have the people you think you need to go forth.

Immediate discouragement comes to your heart when you are at the start, and you don't know everything and have everybody. It is human to feel this way. No rebuke or reprimand; it is just human nature. What do you do? You've got God so you will win the war. You may lose a battle or two, but you will win in the end.

Notes from the Heart

The Heart Thinks

Deuteronomy 4:39 (KJV)
"Know therefore this day, and consider it in thine heart,"

"I'll mull it over and let you know" is a phrase people say when they either don't have an answer or don't want to answer your question or request. You want time to think about it and consider your options, opportunities, and opposite actions.

Your head contains a brain, which is the headquarters of the body, but your thinking, creativity, and incredible mind live in your soul. What if you added the heart to the mix of your thought process? There are some things you decide and do from a heart place that your mind may not understand or agree with.

It doesn't make sense, but it does fire up your passion. It might not make sense, but it does push you to purpose. It might not make sense but it does require your faith.

Don't just think with your head. The scripture says, "Consider it in thine heart." What is the heart saying? It's a sacrifice, but it is worth it. I love it enough to risk it all, and whether I get a return on my investment and risk or not, my heart says to go for it. I'll either be greatly blessed, humbled and compassionate or increase my knowledge and become more teachable.

The heart can help you decide, too, so consider it in your heart.

Remember the heart also thinks.

Notes from the Heart

_____
_____
_____
_____
_____
_____
_____
_____
_____
_____
_____
_____
_____
_____
_____
_____
_____
_____
_____
_____
_____

Notes from the Heart

The Heart Talks

Deuteronomy 7:17 (KJV)
"If thou shalt say in thine **heart**,"

The heart talks, and it talks loudly. It talks loud enough that God hears, understands, and interprets what is happening inside you. My husband often says that my silence speaks very loudly, and he can hear it. Sometimes I want him to hear it, and sometimes I do not. Silence says a lot, and your heart will speak without uttering any words. Our theme scripture says that out of the abundance of the heart, the mouth speaks, and the heart speaks as well. In Deuteronomy, God heard the fear inside of the children of Israel when they were facing their enemies. Their heart said, "We can't win. They are too much for us. We are very afraid." As human beings, we say and feel the exact same way; however, we can't forget that God is with us. So, when your heart says I'm afraid. You agree with it but say back to your heart that we are not going to fear because God is with us. When your heart says, I'm stuck and don't see a way out, which could be true, talk back to the heart. Tell the heart that God IS a way maker. The heart speaks loudly. Talk back to the heart and tell it new words to think, feel, and speak.

Notes from the Heart

Notes from the Heart

Pride in Your Heart

Deuteronomy 8:14 (KJV)
"Then thine **heart** be lifted up,"

You should be proud of yourself, your family, your friends and your accomplishments, but to be lifted up or puffed up in pride is a terrible thing. The heart can be lifted up and forget God. That's horrible pride. This pride is when you get so caught up in yourself you forget God. You forget how He made a way, brought you through, saved your soul, and made you whole. You forget His grace, mercy, and protection through dangers seen and unseen. The heart can oftentimes look through the eyes of achievement and forget to look through the eyes of humility, gratefulness, and submission to God,

His will, and His perfect plan for your life. He spared you. He kept you and never left you. He forgave you. We can do all things through Him. It's in Him we live, move, and have our being.

Reflect, acknowledge and be grateful of all the things God is allowing you to do.

Keep pride out of your heart and Keep God First.

Notes from the Heart

Notes from the Heart

The Heart is Stubborn

Deuteronomy 10:16 (KJV)
"Circumcise therefore the foreskin of your **heart** and be no more stiff-necked."

Determined, driven, persistent, and consistent are words you want to apply to you, your life, and your life's work. There will be times, obstacles, and dilemmas that will enter your life. These things will require you to be determined, diligent, persistent, and consistent until the end. It's a part of life. My grandfather called it having some "grit in your crawl." Don't ask me where it came from but it's all about putting the work in along with great effort. We should all have a little "grit in our crawl," but being stubborn and stiff-necked is something different. Being stubborn is usually associated with an existing problem. Then, someone comes up with a solution with proven facts, testimonials, and statistics that work, but because it's different than what you thought or wanted, you refuse to do it. You won't try it. More importantly, at times, your health is at stake, your livelihood is at stake, and your future is at stake. You won't listen to reason and have made up your mind that you are not going to do what someone else says, even if it could work.

In this scripture, the children of Israel not only had a hard heart, but they were stiff-necked. Their hearts and necks were both stubborn. Additionally, when the scripture says to circumcise their heart, it means to cut, which results in bleeding, hurting, and being sore for a while. After you have healed, God can work with that heart. If your neck is stiff, stuck, and won't move, you can't change directions easily, you can't turn around and see the danger behind you, or only focus on what you want to focus on instead of what God is telling, showing or directing you. Cut off the blockage on your heart and loosen up your neck before you fall, hurt yourself and the next generation.

Notes from the Heart

Gladness of Heart

Deuteronomy 28:47 (KJV)
"Because thou servest not the Lord thy God with joyfulness, and with gladness of heart, for the abundance of all things;"

Psalm 100:2 states that we should "**Serve the LORD with gladness**: come before his presence **with** singing."

In another scripture, it states that God loveth a cheerful giver. If you're doing something unto the Lord, you should be glad, joyful, and happy about it. Don't be mad, irritated, unhappy, or do it out of obligation but, instead be filled with gratitude to serve God. I realize we don't always feel like it, want to, or are happy about the situation. It's because of our flesh that we want something else, spend money or time on something else.

In Deuteronomy, the children of Israel were punished because they didn't serve with gladness and joyfulness unto the Lord especially after all of the things He had done for them. God said, "Since you didn't want to serve me, you'll serve your enemies." Wow, what a turn of events. What a punishment. Being ungrateful, unthankful, and unappreciative would also get you in trouble in my parents' house. There is nothing worse than sacrificing for others, and they don't appreciate it.

Serve the Lord with gladness.

Notes from the Heart

Notes from the Heart

Call the Doctor—The Heart Is Sick

Proverbs 13:12 (KJV)
"Hope deferred maketh the **heart sick**:"

Heart doctors are cardiologists. They can tell by listening to the heart, taking a picture of it, and then making a diagnosis if there is a problem with your heart that needs attention. Proverbs says that hope deferred, delayed, or replaced with anything other than keeping hope alive and thriving will make the heart sick. Why? Hope lives in the heart. You don't hope in your head. You don't hope by what you see. You hope by what's down in your heart. It's the desire, request, and outlook you want for your life that you have hope and it dwells in your heart.

When hope seems to be lost, the heart will be sick. Depression, delays, and denial of a problem will cause the heart to be sick. But the Bible also tells us to hope thou in God, not the things that we see, hear, or know but God.

Keep your heart healthy with hope in God.

Notes from the Heart

Notes from the Heart

Call 911! Now It's the Head and the Heart

Isaiah 1:5 (KJV)

"Why should ye be stricken anymore? Ye will revolt more and more: the whole head is sick, and the whole **heart** faint."

My mama used to say, and still does when we would do something unusual and definitely out of character, "Child, have you lost your mind?" She would also say it about other people, too, "Have they lost their minds?" Some people are just rebellious by nature. It doesn't matter how much you do for them, love them, and seek to guide them; they will go their own way. The children of Israel were no different. The more God brought them out, cared for them, and protected them, the more they still revolted, rebelled, and complained. Their whole head was sick from their way of thinking, processing, and focus. The heart is our seat of passions, desires, and motives. If the head is sick, the heart is faint and not determined to follow God, the punishment and correction will continue. Call 911! The head and the heart are both sick!

Is there a doctor in the house?

Notes from the Heart

Notes from the Heart

Loving With NO Heart

Judges 16:15 (KJV)
"And she said unto him, How canst thou say, I love thee, when thine **heart** is not with me?"

If the heart is the seat where love should live and abide, how can there be love with no heart? You are doing things that love does without the heart attached to it. When you love with your heart, you will stay, abide, work, struggle, and fight when the going gets tough instead of the tough making you go. Loving without your heart's involvement is a matter of duty, like a robot with no feelings. Sure, there are many things we do that are routine—dishes, laundry, serving, cleaning, going to work, pumping gas in the car, washing that same car, and getting oil changes every three months. But we do these routine things because we love our families and want them healthy and safe. Certain routines are a part of life.

You can say the words, "I love you," but if your heart is far, far away from those words. Those are just words without sincerity. Don't forget that God can see the heart and knows its very intent. Your heart is hidden in your chest from the world but not GOD.

This is the commandment that holds all of the laws of the Old Testament, "Love the Lord with All of Your Heart," not words.

Notes from the Heart

_____
_____
_____
_____
_____
_____
_____
_____
_____
_____
_____
_____
_____
_____
_____
_____
_____
_____
_____
_____
_____
_____

Notes from the Heart

The Heart Hears and Decides

Judges 9:3 (KJV)
"And his mother's brethren spake of him in the ears of all the men of Shechem all these words: and their **heart**s inclined to follow Abimelech; for they said, He is our brother."

Perception in the absence of judgment is discernment, a word often used in my home church. You must have a close relationship with God to discern, hear, breakthrough, and get to the core of what is said and done to properly make a decision. Even though the heart is desperately wicked, the heart can also hear what is being said from the unction of the soul. Remember, that is where the will, mind, and emotions live. They all work together. We're listening to what we say to each other with our ears, yet we're discerning, deciding whether to reach out, help, and make connections with our hearts. Our ears, hearts, souls, and spirits all work together, yielding to the Holy Spirit to lead and guide us into all truth.

You know that saying, "something told me." That "something" is the Holy Spirit helping you stay on track, hear God's voice, follow directions, and warning you not to be snared by the devil.

What do you hear?

Notes from the Heart

_____
_____
_____
_____
_____
_____
_____
_____
_____
_____
_____
_____
_____
_____
_____
_____
_____
_____
_____
_____
_____
_____

Notes from the Heart

Comfort Your Heart

2 Thessalonians 2:17 (KJV)
"Comfort your hearts and establish you in every good word and work."

Have you ever been overwhelmed by a project, upcoming event, or simply housework? It can be a combination of many daunting tasks, small details, rising costs, and slow-moving income that bring you to being overwhelmed. The scriptures remind us to comfort our hearts. With what, you might ask? The Word of God. Additionally, add much prayer and your past experiences. Start as early as possible. Break the work up into smaller projects and pieces so you are less overwhelmed. There still maybe much to do, but it is more manageable. When you're overwhelmed, your heart, mind and feet get slowed down. Nothing will get done.

Comfort your heart. Remember what He has already done in and through you. That will be the foundation to establish, stabilize, and progress you in every good work of your hands.

Notes from the Heart

Notes from the Heart

Grieve the Heart

1 Samuel 1:8 (KJV)
"Then said Elkanah, her husband to her, Hannah, why weepest thou? and why eatest thou not? and why is thy **heart** grieved?"

This current generation knows that it wants what it wants. Some are willing to work for it, and some are even willing to hustle. But what happens when you don't get what you want when you want it? Will you be thankful and grateful for the things you already have, or will you make your life and others around you miserable because you don't have what you want?

In the past, I have always heard that Hannah was committed, determined and relentless about her desire for a son. She was willing to do the unorthodox. Hannah sacrificed her time by prayer, supplication, fasting, weeping, and petitioning the Lord for what she wanted—a son. She said in one place, "Give me a son, lest I die." Now that's a serious ask. Her husband was greatly concerned that he was going to lose his wife over a child. He strived to give her everything she ever wanted, but the lack of that one thing caused her heart to grieve. If you're grieving, that means someone or something has died. This is life. The heart can also grieve over something that has not been received, a want, desire or need. Always hope and believe God for anything and everything but if it hasn't happened, surrender to God's will, plan and purpose for your life.

Notes from the Heart

Notes from the Heart

Alot in the Heart

1 Samuel 9:19 (KJV)
"And Samuel answered Saul and said, "I am the seer: go up before me unto the "high place; for ye shall eat with me today, and tomorrow I will let thee go, and will tell thee all that is in thine heart."

Through this study of the heart and writing this book, I found out how much importance God places on the heart, the ways of the heart, and the heart's content. There is a lot to the heart. Sometimes, we don't realize it until we actually speak or even think about something that comes into our heads. We often surprise ourselves by our thoughts and how wicked they really are. Why? We are born in sin, but fortunately, the blood of Jesus cleanses us from the penalty of sin. We still have to fight and die to sin every single day. So, my question today is, what's really down in your heart? It's a lot that could be in your heart, so what really should be there? Take inventory of your heart and give an eviction notice to what doesn't belong there. Only keep what's absolutely necessary and move forward to your purpose and destiny.

Notes from the Heart

Notes from the Heart

Serve With Your Heart

1 Samuel 12:24 (KJV)
"Only fear the Lord, and serve him in truth with all your heart:"

When I was a teenager, I served in many areas of ministry, especially after I received my license to drive. I attended most church activities, sang and directed multiple choirs, ironed uniforms, served in the dining room, and traveled miles to support my pastor and others in music ministry. Not only did I not miss a beat. I had a ball.

In my adult years, I planned local and regional conferences, served on all types of committees, and was on an International Administrative staff for ten years. That opportunity allowed me to travel from one end of the country to the other, serving in ministry. I loved it all! It was different for me because I was an 'all-in girl' who loved the Lord and was taught by my parents to have my own referential fear. I honored the Lord, His house, and His people. My parents and the majority of my family served as role models in front of me, so I followed suit. Now that those role models are no longer around, the gray hairs are scattered throughout my head, and my feet are starting to be strategic about where I will be or go at this stage of life. I still fear the Lord; I want to serve Him in spirit and in truth with my whole heart. My love for God has only grown. I love Him more and more with each passing day.

How will you show up and serve?

Notes from the Heart

Notes from the Heart

_____

_____

_____

_____

_____

_____

_____

_____

_____

_____

_____

_____

_____

_____

_____

_____

_____

_____

_____

_____

_____

The Heart of a Lion

2 Samuel 17:10 (KJV)
"And he also that is valiant, whose **heart** is as the **heart** of a lion, shall utterly melt: for all Israel knoweth that thy father is a mighty man, and they which be with him are valiant men."

No matter how big the other animals are the lion is still king of the jungle. Jesus is the Lamb of God, but in Revelation, Jesus is the one who will open the book because He is the Lion of the tribe of Judah. Words that I would use to characterize the lion are no fear, commands attention, hunter, fighter, protector, and lover.

In 2 Samuel, we see Samuel strived to encourage the children of Israel that God would be on their side. But we are still human beings. Because the most fierce, mighty, valiant warrior with the heart of a lion could also have that same heart melt with fear and having to be reminded that God was with them and would deliver. God is the greatest power, and we shall not be defeated.

You may have the heart of a lion, but greater is He who is with us than he who is against you. Bring it on!

Notes from the Heart

Notes from the Heart

An Understanding Heart

1 Kings 3:12 (KJV)
"Behold, I have done according to thy words: Lo, I have given thee a wise and understanding **heart**;"

There are times when I am trying to explain myself or something to someone and have used the saying, "I'm speaking in English, but you're listening in Russian." Which means that we are not communicating clearly. Truthfully, if we can't understand each other, it will be really hard to stay on the same page and move in the same direction.

There are other times when we use the phrase, "I understand." Do you really understand what's happening, or have you just coined the phrase to make someone feel better? With a wise and understanding heart, you have the wisdom to stop and listen. With an understanding heart, you can choose to empathize, sympathize, or know exactly what that person is going through.

Prior to May of 2010, I could leave my condolences, be in prayer with, and even minister at the funeral for someone who lost a parent. In May of 2010, my father passed away in his sleep. Now, when someone's father passes away, not only do I understand the incident, but feel their pain. I understand from experience and not just a place of empathy. Lord help us all to not only be wise but also with an understanding heart.

Notes from the Heart

Notes from the Heart

After God's Own Heart

1 Samuel 13:14 (KJV)
"But now thy kingdom shall not continue: the Lord hath sought him a man **after** his **own heart**,"

God told Samuel that He rejected the people's pick of Saul to be king. The Lord found a new king for Israel. He was someone of His own choosing and with a heart like His. Wow, what a list of criteria. First of all, to be picked by God was an amazing feat on any level to do anything. Secondly, to realize you have a heart like God's is beyond imagination. Now, only God is perfect, but you want what God wants. You want to feel like God would have you feel. You desire what God wants you to desire. To have a heart like God's or after God's own heart is to have a deep connection with God. That means worshipping Him with your whole heart and wanting to live, be, and do what God wants you to do. Are you perfect? No way. But your heart longs to be what God wants according to His will.

Do you want a heart like God's? Think about it.

Notes from the Heart

Notes from the Heart

_____
_____
_____
_____
_____
_____
_____
_____
_____
_____
_____
_____
_____
_____
_____
_____
_____
_____
_____
_____
_____

A New Heart

Ezekiel 36:26 (KJV)
"A new **heart** also will I give you, and a new spirit will I put within you:"

Dr. Ben Carson has nothing on God for replacing hearts. Without surgery, God can take out your old heart, replace it, mold it, make it, and give you a new heart. If the heart is sick, won't work properly or needs repair or replacement, the whole body won't work right. You don't have the strength, energy, or vitality to do much of anything. You're exhausted all of the time.

In the spiritual realm, with a new heart, you can be used by God for His glory. Your heart has been cleansed, prepared, and ready to be used by God. With a new spirit, you have the power to do it. Put the new heart and the new spirit together, you are dynamite to the Kingdom of God.

Notes from the Heart

Notes from the Heart

A Stony Heart

Ezekiel 36:26 (KJV)
"...I will take away the stony **heart** out of your flesh…"

A rock can be something very small and not much larger than a pebble, but a stone is much larger. In biblical times, people were stoned until they died. Stones have multiple purposes. They can be used to create sturdy, stable shelter us from the elements. A stone can also be used for harm, injury, and ultimately, death.

Ezekiel states that God will take the stony heart of out of your flesh. Supernaturally, God is the surgeon who not only changes your heart but also takes it away and puts a replacement heart inside of you.

In God's eyes, a stony heart cannot be used in His Kingdom. It must go. The stony, unforgiving, cold, hard, and non-compassionate heart must be removed, and something new, fresh, and pliable will be put in its place.

Let God take the stony heart out.

Notes from the Heart

Notes from the Heart

Guard Your Heart

Proverbs 4:23 (NIV)
"Above all else, guard your heart, for everything you do flows from it."

You don't need a guard, lock, or alarm for anything that is NOT valuable. There is an open military base in Texas that does not have guards at the gate. You can just walk or drive on the post and not be stopped or interrupted. There is nothing of great value on that property. On the other hand, at Fort Knox or other active bases, you will be stopped at every turn, and your GPS may not work because they are scrambling signals. Why? There are things, ideas, strategies, and plans that are very valuable to the safety of its personnel on that base. Even physically, your chest cavity has to be broken to do heart surgery. Why? Because your physical heart already has a guard and case around it. There is great value in the heart. The body depends on the heart. No matter how well the other parts of the body are working, if the heart stops, the body stops. If the kidneys stop and the heart is still good, the body can keep going. Proverbs tells us that above everything else, be sure and guard your heart. Protect it. Secure it. Be careful who comes near it or what enters it because everything of value and worth flows out of it.

Security, guard the heart.

Notes from the Heart

_____
_____
_____
_____
_____
_____
_____
_____
_____
_____
_____
_____
_____
_____
_____
_____
_____
_____
_____
_____

Notes from the Heart

Set Your Heart

1 Chronicles 22:19 (KJV)
"Now set your heart..."

I have never been an athlete, yet I love watching great athletes and athletic competitions. When the 100-meter dash or especially the relay races are being run during the Olympics, I'm there. Will they break a record? Who is going to win the race as the fastest man or woman? All of that training for three words: ready, set, and then go. Before you get to go, you have to be set. Being set is being in a position to go. No matter how fast you can run, if you are not set, you won't take off right. You won't have the right foot and balance of your body to run right. I realize that this is practiced over and over again so that they can run properly. If someone starts before the gun goes off, you have to go back, you get a warning and start over. If someone appears to be set but hesitates just a little, they won't have a great race either. Is your heart really set on the things you are spending so much energy doing? Are you sure this is really what God called you to do? Not saying that it is a bad thing, but it may not be the GOD thing He has called you to do. Once your heart is set, no matter what people say or do, you are going to do what God called you, trained you, equipped you, and gifted you to do. Are you ready? Now get set. Go and don't look back until you finish.

Notes from the Heart

Notes from the Heart

An Undivided Heart

1 Chronicles 28:9 (GNT])
"And to Solomon he said, "My son, I charge you to acknowledge your father's God and to serve him with an undivided **heart** and a willing mind."

Solomon's father advised his son, "to serve God with your whole heart and a willing mind." Dividing a pizza is great to be shared with friends. Peeling and dividing an orange makes a sweet piece of fruit last longer, however, a divided heart gets nothing accomplished. Why? Because you can't make a decision. Even if you are forced to decide to pick a side, you're not fully all in. It's only a partial commitment or a half-hearted effort. You are not giving your best self to the idea, the project, the life, the career, or to God. More importantly, God knows it even if you don't want to admit it because He sees your heart. It's still your choice. The best relationships, quality of life, and abundant life come from willingly giving God your whole heart. He loves you enough to create circumstances and events that compel and lovingly drive you back to Him.

Come willingly, on your own and with your whole heart.

Notes from the Heart

Notes from the Heart

An Unprepared Heart

2 Chronicles 12:14 (KJV)
"And he did evil because he prepared not his **heart** to seek the Lord."

As an educator, singer, speaker and coach, there is nothing worse than not only the feeling but reality of being unprepared. It throws everything off. Sure, you can get yourself together and do it in a pinch or on short notice; however, for me, not being prepared feels like waking up from a nightmare. I would rather be over-prepared than not prepared at all. When you are not prepared, you are subject to do things, say things, and make decisions that can be detrimental to the assignment, whole project and career. It can have an impact on future opportunities and set you back in your professional development, growth and expansion. People won't be able to count on you. You weren't prepared and you may not complete the task at hand.

In this scripture, the person did evil because he did not prepare his heart. Fixing his heart or setting his heart to seek God was not part of his plan. When you don't seek God, you are subject to take advice from anybody. You do things that are totally out of character which can re-directing your path and destiny. God is not surprised. Others may be surprised. You didn't seek wise counsel. You didn't ask God. If you asked, you didn't obey what God said. Remember, seek ye first. Prayer, Permission and Preparation are crucial to success.

These steps will lead to a prepared heart. Once you've received God's instruction and in spite of how you feel or how it looks, God's perfect plan, will and purpose for your life will make it all worth.

Prepare your heart and watch God order your steps.

Notes from the Heart

The Heart of the King

Proverbs 21:1 (KJV)
"The king's **heart** is in the hand of the Lord, as the rivers of water: he turneth it whithersoever he will."

When I think of kings in the Bible, I think of King Saul, King David and Queen Esther's husband, King Ahasuerus. King David was a man after God's heart. I truly believe that God clearly turned the heart of King Ahasuerus with the beauty, advice, and obedience of Queen Esther. Although Queen Esther sought the advice of her uncle, Mordecai, it was her willingness to fast, pray, and create a tribe of intercessors with her handmaidens and other servants that caused their petitions for the children of Israel to bombard heaven. Favor, persuasion, and action caused the heart of the king to be turned to the benefit of God's people.

What do you need God to do for you? Who do you need God to work on, work through, and work with to get it done? It does not matter how evil, determined, and unrelenting the supervisor, boss, or CEO is. If it's God's will, their heart will be turned in your favor, and your petition will be granted.

The heart of the King is still in God's hands.

Notes from the Heart

Notes from the Heart

The Heart That Lives Forever

Psalm 22:26 (KJV)
"The meek shall eat and be satisfied: they shall praise the LORD that seek him: your **heart** shall live forever."

The word meek is defined as humbly patient or quiet in nature. The synonyms for meek are soft, overly submissive, or tamed. That sounds like a pushover or someone who doesn't have much initiative or motivation. But in actuality, meekness is not the same as weakness. It takes strength, courage and wisdom to be meek. The synonym of tamed or overly submissive may sound like weakness but it is actually discipline. Knowing when to submit and when to rise up is actually power and control. Some fights you aren't meant to fight. God will fight for you and supply all of your needs and you will be satisfied. The meek will praise the Lord, serve Him, and obey Him, their hearts will live forever.

Remember, blessed are the pure in heart, for they shall see God. I believe we will see His works, benefits, and blessings on Earth and in Heaven. Give no thought about how your meekness looks to men, praise the Lord and keep going because He will provide. Your physical heart and body will die here on earth, but the meek shall live forever in God's presence.

Notes from the Heart

Notes from the Heart

The Troubled Heart

Psalm 25:17 (KJV)
"The troubles of my **heart** are enlarged: O bring thou me out of my distresses."

When you're in trouble, you just want one thing, and that is for that trouble to end. In this Psalm, the troubles and struggles are not only present, but they have grown or gotten bigger. In the TikTok world, "it got worser." It is one thing for trouble to come and another thing for that trouble to get worse before it gets better.

I heard a mother on the phone with her child repeating, "Don't get into any more trouble." She was loud; I didn't have to eavesdrop to hear or know that the child had been in trouble and she was trying to stop it from getting worse.

For trouble to get on the inside of your heart is another level of trouble. The trouble of and in the heart keep you up at night. It causes worry and a lack of focus on the tasks at hand. As a woman, I am always striving to find solutions to the trouble. I want to fix it and get it over with.

Sometimes there is a lesson or a reason for the trouble. I always pray that I learn the lessons, remember them, and work extremely hard to not repeat them.

I want God to bring me out of any trouble I am in. Why? In the words of my mother, "God can work that thing out so smooth, clean, and better than anyone else." If your heart is troubled, give it to God so He can give you, His peace. Give it to

God and He'll take out the stress and bring you out alright.

Notes from the Heart

The Strengthened Heart

Psalm 27:14 (KJV)
"Wait on the LORD: be of good courage, and he shall strengthen thine **heart**: wait, I say, on the LORD."

The strengthening of the heart comes from three things in the scripture: God, waiting, and trusting. These are the powerful elements of a strengthened, mature heart because God is the only one who knows the heart better than any doctor in the world. Being of good courage is "standing on business," as the young people say. This means trusting that God is going to do what He said. Your courage only comes through knowing that God can do anything. Your past experience with God is your evidence. He is not a one-hit wonder; He has done it before, and He will do it again. He may not do it the same way, with the same person, or with the same result; just trust that He will get it fixed!

Ultimately, the most difficult part is waiting on the Lord. As human beings, this is the hardest part. We never know how long we are going to have to wait. Sometimes, we don't know exactly what we're waiting on. Finally, we don't know how the situation is going to change or worsen until the Lord shows up on our behalf.

The psalmist said, "Wait on the Lord" twice. The second time, he emphasizes "I say," then finishes with "on the Lord." Hear me clearly and do exactly what I say because it will bless you. Your heart will be strengthened by the Lord if you

WAIT and take courage by trusting in the one who CAN do it—God.

Notes from the Heart

The Designer Heart

Psalm 33:15 (KJV)
"He fashioneth their **heart**s alike; he considereth all their works."

Most of us just dream about designer clothing. The price of the clothing will limit our access. Did I mention the price? That alone stops many of us from purchasing. Because my father was so short, he wore tailor-made suits. For a college graduation gift, he had his tailor fit me for two suits—a reddish, maroon-colored suit and a black pinstripe suit. I was in heaven. Why? Because the suits were made explicitly for me, my height, size, arm length, shoulder length, and everything in between. The tailor measured me from head to toe and even embroidered my name on the satin lining inside suit coat jackets. I love those suits and still have them to this day. I can't tell you how many boxes, miles traveled, different cities and closets those suits have hung in. They were customized especially for me. Someone would have to have the suits resized or remade to fit their body. The suits were made especially for me. My father considered the places I would go, the people I would meet and determined that I needed clothing fashioned for those occasions. He wanted me to fit in with not only my knowledge but also my appearance.

Our Heavenly Father is no different. He has fashioned our hearts through our experiences, personalities, and passions to be able to do the work He called us to do. You are a designer original with the heart for it. You have the knowledge, spirit, and strength from God to carry out His plan for your life. He has even embroidered His name on your heart.

Notes from the Heart

The Law Is in the Heart

Psalm 40:8 (KJV)
"I delight to do thy will, O my God: yea, thy law is within my **heart**."

Why is it not hard to do thy will? Because the law of God is in my heart. The law is God's Word. The psalmist says that he even takes delight in doing God's will because God's law is within his heart. How did it get there? You have to put the law in your heart daily. In fact, you have to continue to put it there weekly, hourly, and sometimes on a minute-by-minute basis. You have to read it, sing it, and meditate on it day and night. It just doesn't happen overnight. God's Word, the law, must become routine and methodical. You must make it a part of your daily nourishment.

David said, "It is as necessary or even more necessary than daily food." Why? Life is hard. The song says, Life is filled with swift transition…" Meaning life will change, switch and be totally different very quickly. However, you don't have to look up anything, call someone, or fight this fight without ammunition because your ammunition is the Word of God.

Fast, quick, and in a hurry, you have to remind your heart what God's Word says, what God promised, and what God has already done in the past. With that knowledge in the database down in your heart, you are equipped to move forward. What did you read today?

Notes from the Heart

Notes from the Heart

A Fixed Heart

Psalm 57:7 (KJV)
"My **heart** is fixed, O God, my **heart** is fixed: I will sing and give praise."

I hate to get lost. I don't like anything broken around me. Fix it or throw it out! I shut down when we can't make a plan or decision on how to fix something. Once I know the plan, solution or strategy, I'm all in to help get it fixed. The psalmist is clear and even repeats that "my heart is fixed." This sounds like a person with determination, decisiveness, vision, and a clear direction of where they are going. To top it all off, the psalmist is giving, praising, and singing unto God with a fixed heart.

Why? Because he knows that God is his help, source and solution to every situation. Therefore, his heart can be fixed, not broken or undecided because he knows the power of his God.

Celebrate your decision and the God of that decision with a fixed heart.

Notes from the Heart

Notes from the Heart

The Broken Heart

> Psalm 147:3 (KJV)
> "He healeth the broken in heart, and bindeth up their wounds."

A broken heart can happen to people in so many ways. Normally, we think of a heartbreak in a love relationship and there have been millions of songs written about love heart break. But a broken heart is associated with more than just a love relationship. A broken heart can happen within every facet of life's situations and circumstances. A broken heart can stem from disappointment and the unrealized potential on so many levels.

You invested a lot into the plan, project or person. You were all in, but you couldn't get the capital loan, someone took your idea and launched before you could get it off the ground or you couldn't get anyone to see the vision and buy in. You may be discouraged and feel like a failure.

Maybe you suffered the loss of a loved one and the grief journey has been too much and you're overwhelmed with sorrow.

Your heart may be broken for any number of reasons. But I have good news.

God can heal your broken heart

This Psalm states that God can heal the brokenhearted if you will let Him. He will bind up, heal, restore, and recover your injured wounds. The heart is precious and fragile. It can easily be broken but it will require the hands of the Almighty

God to put all of the broken pieces of your heart back together again.

Notes from the Heart

About the Author

Julia Royston spends her days doing what she loves, writing, publishing, speaking about her why and motto, "Helping You Get Your Message to the Masses, Turn Your Words into Wealth and Be a Book Business Boss." Julia is the author of 120+ books, Co-Authored 9 books, published 400+, recorded 3 music CDs and coached more than 250+ to be published authors.

She is the owner of five companies, a non-profit organization and the editor of the Book Business Boss Magazine.

To stay connected with Julia, visit www.juliaakroyston.com.

Social Media

Facebook - @juliaaroyston

IG - @juliaaroyston

LinkedIN - @juliaaroyston

TikTok - @juliaaroyston

More Books by this Author

www.ingramcontent.com/pod-product-compliance
Lightning Source LLC
Chambersburg PA
CBHW071205160426
43196CB00011B/2199